# Time Management: How to Manage Your Time, Be More Productive, and Overcome Procrastination

By Dominic Mann

# Table of Contents

# Introduction

The Roman Republic was founded in 509 BC. At the time, it was no more than a small city. However, by the time the Roman Republic transformed itself into the Roman Empire, it controlled the entire Mediterranean, all of continental Europe, as well as parts of Asia, Africa, and England.

This begs the question, how did this little city conquer the world? How did they go from relative insignificance to dominating three continents?

More importantly, what can we learn from them? How can we achieve similarly jaw-dropping results in our own lives?

At the core of it all is productivity.

Productivity means getting more done. Whether that be conquering the world or conquering your to-do list, a little extra productivity never hurts.

To understand the secret to the astounding military success of the Romans, we must first understand the three dimensions of productivity. Here they are:

1. Time
2. Speed
3. Efficiency

In other words, there are three avenues through which you can increase productivity. You can work longer (i.e. increase time). You can work harder (i.e. increase speed). You can work smarter (i.e. increase efficiency). Time, speed, and efficiency.

Now, back to the Romans.

Working longer wasn't an option for the Romans. All of their enemies had the exact same 24 hours each day. It would be impossible to outwork them. At best, they could hope to match them, but that's no winning strategy.

Working harder wasn't an option for the Romans either. Battle is a matter of life and death, and so both sides fight with just as much vigor as the other. Once again, they could match their enemies in this respect, but not surpass them. No winning strategy here.

To maximize results, the only avenue available to the Romans was to work smarter. And this they did. They became ridiculously efficient.

In battle, the barbarians had large, intimidating weapons. Big battle axes. Long swords. Scary stuff meant for hacking, chopping, and slicing and dicing enemy soldiers.

The Romans, on the other hand, went with a little, short, pointed, dagger-like sword called the gladius. It was terrible at chopping and slicing. Compared to the terrifying weapons wielded by the barbarian hordes, the gladius seemed like a kid's toy. Nonetheless, the gladius' small six inch point consistently beat the enemy — even though the enemy wielded significantly more fearsome weapons.

The tiny gladius was able to repeatedly deal the enemy massive defeats not despite its small size, but because of its small size!

Swinging big, long, heavy weapons is exhausting. Furthermore, all that wild flailing around frequently leaves one exposed just long enough for a Roman to thrust his gladius from behind a wall of shields.

While the opposing barbarians were working incredibly hard, the Romans barely broke a sweat. This ruthlessly efficient strategy saved the Romans much effort, giving them the energy to fight several times longer than the enemy.

By working smart, the Romans doubled — even tripled — their odds of victory. And that's what this book is all about. Working smarter and more efficiently. Maximizing results through the intelligent application of time management strategies. Getting more done without working 20 hours a day or consuming Red Bull by the truckload.

Strategy is the key to effective time management. Just as a general can conquer foreign lands by strategically deploying troops, you can conquer your to-do list with strategic time management.

Bruce Lee once said, "If you love life, don't waste time, for time is what life is made up of."

As if replying to Lee's insight, Peter Drucker said, "Until we can manage time, we can manage nothing else."

To live the life we want, we must know how to manage our time. So let's dive right in and discover how.

# Chapter 1: Divide and Conquer

Tasks, like armies, are easier to conquer if divided. Cut-throat efficiency requires the disassembly of goals into bite-sized chunks.

Unfortunately, most people utilize only two of the three dimensions of productivity: Time and speed. They work long and they work hard. They boast of 100 hour work weeks and brag of surviving on no more than four hours sleep a night. Their cupboards are full of coffee and their playlists full of motivational videos.

All of this can help boost productivity in the short-term, but it leaves the most important component of productivity unused: Efficiency. They work long and hard, but all too often they don't work smart. They are astonishingly busy yet accomplish shockingly little. They're like a hurricane. Like an uncoordinated riot. Like a leaderless movement. There is much motion but little accomplishment. As Benjamin Franklin said, "Never confuse motion with action."

Peak productivity requires the utilization of all three dimensions of productivity: Time, speed, and efficiency. And one of the best ways to increase efficiency is to break tasks down into little steps. Victory is made easier, and conquering more effortless, when the enemy's forces (i.e. your task or project) are divided into little chunks that can be defeated piecemeal.

Small chucks of food are more easily digested. Fractured cubes of ice are quicker to melt. So too are projects divided into small steps more efficiently completed.

## Maximizing Every Moment

Much like a handful of nuts or a bag of chips, bite-sized tasks can be nibbled on at random times.

Left with a spare moment because a meeting finished early and there's another one straight after? One of your coworkers says, "Well, we've got eight minutes. Any of you watch 'The Bachelor' finale last night?" What a waste of time.

By breaking larger tasks down into little steps, odd moments like this can become highly productive. Like a bag of salted nuts, they can be snacked upon at random times, leaving you with a well gobbled up to-do list at the day's end.

Similarly, just as unappetizing foods are easier contemplated in small serves, tedious tasks are easier begun when broken down into small, actionable steps. Rather than torturing yourself with the thought of writing that entire 1,000 word article, focus on its components. Break it down into small steps. Focus on writing just the first five words.

## Procrastination Termination

*"The journey of a thousand miles begins with one step."*
— *Lao Tzu*

Feeling overwhelmed is one the main reasons people procrastinate. When things are getting difficult and boring with no satisfaction or sense of achievement in sight, procrastination is easily succumbed to. Breaking down larger tasks and projects into small steps keeps a constant flow of satisfaction.

You achieve the first step — yay! — and that feeling of achievement spurs you on to complete yet another one, and another, and another one. It builds momentum like a snowball rolling down a hill.

Speaking of momentum, here is Newton's first law:

*"Every object persists in its state of rest or uniform motion in a straight line unless it is compelled to change that state by forces impressed on it."*

In other words, objects at rest remain at rest and objects in motion remain in motion. That's why if you hit a golf ball in space, it would continue flying through space forever. Likewise, if you put a golf ball in space and left it there, it would stay there forever.

Newton's first law also applies to procrastination. After all, objects at rest tend to stay at rest.

The good news, however, is that objects in motion stay in motion. That's why you hear so much talk of developing a powerful morning routine. If you start the day strong, that momentum continues all day — just like a golf ball flying through outer space.

As Newton's first law makes clear, the most important thing is to just get started. This is, once again, why breaking larger tasks down into little steps is so effective. It allows you to quickly and easily get started on things, building momentum which continues to propel you on and on.

So break down larger tasks into unintimidating small steps. Procrastination will become less tempting and momentum will be generated.

<u>Results Oriented</u>

*"Stressing output is the key to improving productivity, while looking to increase activity can result in just the opposite."*
— *Paul Gauguin*

Breaking projects down to their basic components ensures that every action you take is moving you toward your end goal. The division between that which moves you toward your goal (taking action on those "little steps") and that which doesn't move you toward your goal becomes increasingly clear. You gain newfound clarity regarding what needs to be done and what achieves nothing. Between that which is productive and unproductive.

### Stress Drops, Focus Soars

*"Your mind is for having ideas, not holding them."*
— *David Allen*

In his bestselling book, *Getting Things Done*, David Allen argues that moving planned tasks out of the mind by writing them down frees you to focus on taking action rather than trying to remember all what needs to be done.

Allen also makes the case that reverse engineering tasks and projects into actionable work items amplifies this effect by allowing you to focus solely on taking action. Instead of thinking, "What should I do now?" you're gobbling down bite-sized capsules of ultra-productive work.

## All in All

Dividing large tasks up into little steps not only makes your workflow more efficient, but it enables you to utilize small blocks of time that would otherwise be wasted.

Additionally, little steps enable you to quickly get started without feeling overwhelmed. This reduces the allure of tempting distractions and helps build momentum, putting the full force of Newton's first law and the snowball effect behind you.

Finally, this approach to time management ensures that all of your actions are whisking you toward your goal. This means you end up less stressed and are better able to focus solely on taking action.

# Chapter 2: The McDonald's System

*"We should work on our process, not the outcome of our process."*
— *W. Edwards Deming*

McDonald's has 36,525 restaurants around the globe. They are found in 118 countries and serve 68 million customers each day. That's around one percent of world's population, every single day. Mind blowing.

McDonald's employs half a million people, most of whom, as you probably know, are acne-ridden high school kids.

But here is the most amazing part: Despite the massive scale and complexity of this multinational corporation, their product and service is consistent.

I could go to a McDonald's store in the United States, then the United Kingdom, and then in Australia, and everything would be the same. I would get the same food. I would get the same service. The store would look the same. Everything.

Even more staggering is that most McDonald's employees are failing high school students.

How is it that McDonald's, in all its 36,525 stores, is perfectly consistent — especially when its employees are mostly incompetent?

Here's how: McDonald's has a secret. They are perhaps the best in the world at creating systems. They break down all aspects of the business into their simplest components. They reduce their entire business to no more than a collection of little steps. They make these small steps so simple that a bunch of failing high school kid can run the business. Literally.

McDonald's builds a simple, step by step process. They then turn it over to their employees. The result of this system is that you get the exact same experience no matter what McDonald's store you go to — an extraordinarily impressive feat considering they hire some of the least skilled workers in the world.

So let's take a look at what the "McDonald's system" can teach us about time management.

The General and the Troops

Most people work long and hard, but fail to work smart. The biggest hurdle to working smart is indecision and lack of direction. This is because we humans have two modes of work: Strategizing and doing. We plan and we act.

The problem is that we often try to do both of these things at the same time. One minute we are in "go mode," the next minute we are in "strategy mode." This not only slows us down and makes us highly inefficient, but it leads to multitasking and decision fatigue.

Multitasking causes a 40 percent drop in efficiency. Decision fatigue depletes one's willpower. Decision fatigue also, as its name suggests, reduces the quality of subsequent decisions.

So what's the solution?

This dilemma can be resolved by dedicating a block of time to being in "strategy mode." This frees up the rest of one's time for being in "go mode." This clear division eliminates the need for multitasking. It also extinguishes the decision fatigue that saps at one's willpower and reduces the quality of one's work.

The effectiveness of an army would be severely limited if men were required to fill both the role of the general and the infantry.

The quality of an essay would be severely limited if one could not draw up an outline.

The insight offered by an academic paper would be severely limited were it not researched and planned.

The potential success of a business would be severely limited if no business plan were to be produced.

The ability of a film to engage and captivate audiences would be severely limited if the director had no script.

The safety of passenger jets would be severely limited if pilots never had takeoff checklists.

The utility of an airplane as a method of transport would be severely limited were there no flight plans.

It's clear, isn't it? "Strategy mode" and "go mode" must be disentangled from one another. One cannot direct a film without already having a script. One cannot write an effective academic paper without prior research and planning. One cannot be both general and soldier.

To maximize efficiency, one must set aside a block of time dedicated to being the general — "strategy mode." Then one can return to the battlefield as a soldier — "go mode" — free of strategy-related worries.

By disentangling these two roles, one can mindlessly power through stacks of complex work without so much as a single thought. This is efficiency at its best. It's the beauty of working smart.

As success coach Brian Tracy said, "Every minute you spend in planning saves 10 minutes in execution; this gives you a 1,000 percent Return on Energy!"

You can't be both CEO and employee at the same time. You can't be both general and soldier at the same time. Separate the two roles and your efficiency will go through the roof. You must work smart.

## Utilizing the Process

The first step to utilizing the "McDonald's system" is to set aside one day each week for intense planning. You will spend this time planning the week or so.

Although it might seem rather extreme to be spending this much time on planning, remember that the more detail that goes into planning, the less time you will end up wasting during the week. As Brian Tracy said in the aforementioned quote, "Every minute you spend in planning saves 10 minutes in execution." Sounds like a good deal to me.

Furthermore, you will eventually become faster. You'll end up being able to plan the next week in a single afternoon (or evening) at the end of the weekend.

Keep in mind that it is important to not include any more than five major goals or projects.

Now, the second step is to break these goals into smaller tasks — sub-projects.

For the third step, make sure to go into "McDonald's level" detail on your sub-projects. Make it so simple that an ance-ridden failing high school kid could do it. You want to make it so that you don't have to think about what it is that you're doing. You can just go, go, go without needing to stop and think too much. You want to work with machine-like efficiency.

The fourth step is to determine how long each task will take and assign time frames. It might take an entire day, half a day, or a quarter of a day. Be a little conservative. It's better to have a little time left over than to be forced to completely abandon your plan.

Finally, the fifth step is to print your plan out and stick it to your desk. This plan is to you what a map is to a sailor. With this plan, you'll be free to focus exclusively on taking action — being in "go mode" — for the next week or so. No more worrying about what the next step is or constantly switching between "strategy mode" and "go mode."

By embracing the "McDonald's system" and disentangling the roles of general and soldier, you eliminate decision fatigue, boost energy levels, and skyrocket your efficiency.

The creation of such a roadmap by laying out the process — the little steps — enables clockwork-like productivity. Just like in a mechanical clock, all the little parts work together to create a perfectly predictable outcome.

<u>Process vs Outcome</u>

There two ways one can operate:

1. Focus on the outcome.
2. Focus on the process.

As you likely know, most people focus exclusively on the outcome. This can be handy in "strategy mode," however, if it persists throughout other stages of work — such as "go mode" — this obsessive focus on the outcome can, ironically, become detrimental to the outcome.

Measuring yourself against short-term results is a terrible strategy. The key to effective time management and the consequent jaw-dropping productivity is to determine the actions that lead to the long-term results you desire.

Focus on the process, not the outcome. You have zero control over the outcome. What you do have control over, however, is the process. Adjust the process and the results you are getting will change accordingly. Just focusing on the outcome will not move you any nearer to that which you are striving for.

# Chapter 3: Daily Planning

*"He who every morning plans the transaction of the day and follows out that plan, carries a thread that will guide him through the maze of the most busy life. But where no plan is laid, where the disposal of time is surrendered merely to the chance of incidence, chaos will soon reign."*
*— Victor Hugo*

The habit of daily planning ensures that you are always in control. For this reason, it is a highly effective time management tool. As former Prime Minister of Israel, Golda Meir, said, "I must govern the clock, not be governed by it."

## Proactive, Not Reactive

*"It had long since come to my attention that people of accomplishment rarely sat back and let things happen to them. They went out and happened to things."*
*— Leonardo da Vinci*

Most people roll out of bed, landing on the floor with a heavy thud. One would imagine that a corpse falling off a trolley in the morgue would sound much the same.

They then realize that they're late, yet again! That damn snooze button. With bleary-eyes and a skyrocketing heart rate, they race down the stairs in panic. No time for breakfast.

A short while later, they are stuck in traffic, bumper-to-bumper with tens of thousands of other mediocre morons just like them. As they all go about sipping on their shitty convenience store coffee, they shout and swear at each other.

This reactive state of mind continues for the rest of the day. And then the next. And the next. And the next.

The problem with this is that they react to things rather than create things. They are not in control, and that is no way to go about time management.

If all you do is react to things as they happen to you, time management is impossible. What you need to do is be proactive. You need to take control of your time and work toward meaningful goals that you have set yourself, rather than just reacting to external things like emails, calls, coworkers, requests, and so on. Be proactive, not reactive.

Instead of merely treading water (i.e. being reactive), decide upon a destination and start swimming there.

The Ivy Lee Method

*"Never begin a day until it is finished on paper."*
— *Jim Rohn*

In 1918, Charles M. Schwab was president of the Bethlehem Steel Corporation. Under his leadership, the Bethlehem Steel Corporation became the world's largest independent steel producer and the largest shipbuilder in America at the time. This massive success made Schwab one of the world's richest men.

Thomas Edison gave some insight into the reasons for Schwab's staggering success when he referred to him as the "master hustler." Schwab was always seeking ways through which he could get an edge over his competition.

In his search for that extra competitive edge, Schwab had a meeting with Ivy Lee, a highly respected productivity consultant. Schwab wanted to know if there was anything he could do to increase his team's efficiency and get things done better.

So Schwab challenged Lee, "Show me a way to get more things done with my time and I'll pay you any fee within reason."

Lee handed Schwab a piece of blank paper. Lee told him to write down, each evening, the things he needed to do the next day. Schwab was then told to number these tasks in order of importance. The next morning, these tasks were to be completed in that exact order. Task number one had to be done before moving onto task number two. The same for tasks number three, four, and so on.

On his blog (http://jamesclear.com/), James Clear suggests that Ivy Lee also told Schwab to list no more than six tasks. This is undoubtedly an excellent idea as it keeps one focused on only the most important things that need to be accomplished. Such focus leads to higher efficiency and better quality work. As the great Roman philosopher Seneca once said, "To be everywhere is to be nowhere." If you're being pulled in all directions, you remain stationary. Focus is key.

Finally, Ivy Lee said, "Don't worry if you don't complete everything on the schedule. At least you will have completed the most important projects before getting to the less important ones."

Ivy Lee then had a bunch of 15 minute meetings with each of Schwab's executives, telling them to do the same.

Schwab offered to pay Lee for his services, but Lee declined. Lee simply told Schwab that, after three months, he could send a check for whatever he felt it was worth to him.

When all was done and dusted, Schwab sent Lee a $25,000 check, the equivalent of $400,000 in today's money. He later credited Lee with having given him the most profitable lesson of his entire business career -- quite a claim coming from someone of such immense wealth.

So start each and every day by doing the most important thing. Then, do the second most important thing. Then the third. It's one of the most effective — and, as Schwab can attest to, profitable — productivity hacks you'll ever learn.

## The ABC Method

*"The law of Forced Efficiency says that 'There is never enough time to do everything, but there is always enough time to do the most important thing.' Put another way, you cannot eat every tadpole and frog in the pond, but you can eat the biggest and ugliest one, and that will be enough, at least for the time being."*
— *Brian Tracy, Eat That Frog!*

Success coach Brian Tracy devised a productivity system similar to the one Ivy Lee taught Charles Schwab.

Tracy advises that each morning or evening, create a to-do list for the day ahead. Once you're finished, put your tasks into three categories: "A", "B", and "C".

"A" tasks are your most important tasks.

"B" tasks are your kind of important tasks. Someone might get annoyed if you don't do them, but they are not as important as your "A" tasks.

"C" tasks are non-essential tasks such as reading the news or doing personal business during work hours.

Once you've categorized your tasks in this way, you number the tasks by importance in each category. This will give you "A1", "A2", and so on. The same goes for "B" and "C" tasks with "B1", "B2", and so on.

Now, Tracy advises that we do these tasks in that exact order. Starting with the "A1" task and not moving on until it is complete. Same goes with the rest of the tasks — for example, no doing "B" tasks until all the "A" tasks are complete.

The productivity system's of both Brian Tracy and Ivy Lee both share one thing in common: They require you to complete tasks in order of their importance. This way, you do all the hard tasks while you're motivated, rested, and refreshed, while doing the easier tasks after that "post-lunch slump." Moreover, even if you don't complete all the tasks, you will have nonetheless completed the most important, profitable activities. So even on your worst days, you're still killing it!

# Chapter 4: Scheduling Your Priorities

*"The key is not to prioritize what's on your schedule, but to schedule your priorities."*
*— Stephen Covey, The 7 Habits of Highly Effective People*

*"The main thing is to keep the main thing the main thing." — Stephen Covey, The 7 Habits of Highly Effective People*

*"Fix your ideal schedule, then work backwards to make everything fit — ruthlessly culling obligations, turning people down, becoming hard to reach, and shedding marginally useful tasks along the way. My experience in trying to make that fixed schedule a reality forces any number of really smart and useful in-the-moment productivity decisions."*
*— Cal Newport*

The Eisenhower Matrix

*"What is important is seldom urgent and what is urgent is seldom important."*

*— Dwight D. Eisenhower, 34th President of the United States*

A Jedi master named Steve has just discovered that the love of his life is about to be burned to little more than a pile of ash. Princess Luna is trapped inside of a burning building.

To save his princess from premature cremation, Steve rushes off to save her. To his horror, he is intercepted by a hostile swarm of Stormtroopers who are set on destroying him. They open fire, sending laser bullets screaming through the air.

Much to Steve's dismay, he is forced to constantly dodge the gleaming laser bullets that are attempting to extinguish his life. If he gets hit — poof — he's gone.

Steve immediately realizes that he's stuck with a terrible dilemma. If he spends time fighting the never ending army of stormtroopers, his princess will be consumed by hungry flames.

While Steve could temporarily fight off the gathering hordes of Stormtroopers, he would fail to achieve his main objective: Saving his beloved Princess Luna.

The choice becomes clear: That which is urgent versus that which is important.

The stormtroopers are urgent, but not important. Saving Princess Luna is important, but not quite as urgent.

As Eisenhower said, "What is important is seldom urgent and what is urgent is seldom important."

Every day, we are faced with this exact dilemma. Like Steve, we have things which are urgent, but not important. Our very own stormtroopers. We also have things which are important, but not urgent. The Princess Lunas of our lives. Unfortunately, the urgent yet unimportant stormtroopers of our lives hold us back. As Eisenhower said in the aforementioned quote, "What is important is seldom urgent." Thus, we end up erroneously prioritizing the stormtroopers over our Princess Lunas. A very sad dilemma indeed.

The solution to this sad dilemma is hidden between the lines of Eisenhower's insightful words. We must constantly remind ourselves what is truly important. Whether it be exercise and family versus Facebook notifications and news alerts, or long-term professional goals versus productivity-sapping email.

Inspired by Eisenhower's way of thinking, a great time management tool known as the "Eisenhower Matrix" was born.

Here's how it works.

First, you draw up a box with four squares. Basically a big plus (i.e. "+") symbol inside a square. On top of this two-by-two table, you write "Urgent" above the first column and "Not Urgent" above the second column. On the side of the table, you write "Important" next to the top row and "Not Important" next to the bottom row.

The result is that there will be a square for each of the following categories of tasks:

- Urgent and important
- Important, but not urgent
- Urgent, but not important
- Neither urgent nor important

Furthermore, tasks will be responded to differently depending on the category they fit. For example, tasks that are both urgent and important will be done immediately. Important tasks that are not urgent will be scheduled to be done later. Urgent tasks that are not important will be delegated to someone else. And, finally, tasks that are neither urgent nor important will be eliminated.

The Eisenhower Matrix is an incredibly effective time management tool because it invariably forces you to focus only on the things that are most important. As a result, you make rapid progress on your biggest, most ambitious, most important goals.

You also become increasingly efficient as you eliminate unimportant tasks and focus exclusively on the ultra-profitable few. You do more of that which delivers the results you desire, financial or otherwise.

## First Things First

*"The main thing is to keep the main thing the main thing."*
— *Stephen Covey*

In his book, *The 7 Habits of Highly Effective People*, Stephen Covey advises that we "put first things first," listing this as the third habit of highly effective people. The single biggest hurdle to peak productivity is the failure to put first things first and keep the main thing the main thing.

I'll repeat that again as it is so very important: The single biggest hurdle to peak productivity is the failure to put first things first. In other words, the failure to keep the main thing the main thing.

There is a massive discrepancy between people's words and people's actions. They say they prioritize family and health, and yet they go home after work and watch television, eat unhealthy pre-packaged meals, and mindlessly scroll through their Facebook news feed. So much for family and health, right?

There is a difference between what their words say are their "first things" (i.e. family and health in this example), and what their actions say are their "first things" (i.e. watching television and reading Facebook in this example). As such, this person obviously isn't putting "first things first."

We need to keep first things first.

Similarly, we need to keep the main thing the main thing. Too often we get bogged down by distractions and quickly find that we've lost sight of our "main thing."

Most people fail to keep the main thing the main thing.

### Romans on the Shortness of Life

*"It is not that we have so little time but that we lose so much. ... The life we receive is not short but we make it so; we are not ill provided but use what we have wastefully."*
— *Seneca, On the Shortness of Life*

*"People are frugal in guarding their personal property; but as soon as it comes to squandering time they are most wasteful of the one thing in which it is right to be stingy."*
— *Seneca, On the Shortness of Life*

Over 2,000 years ago, living during the time of the Roman Empire, a Roman philosopher by the name of Seneca wrote an essay, *On the Shortness of Life*. In this essay, Seneca makes the argument that life is not too short, despite most people complaining otherwise.

He argues, much like Stephen Covey does in *The 7 Habits of Highly Effective People*, that people spend most of their time doing unimportant things.

In today's society, Seneca would likely refer to such things as the excessive — no, more like wasteful — amount of time most people spend on email when it's not necessary, mindlessly browsing Facebook, watching television, and so on. In fact, he'd probably also argue against the biggest time waster of all: Working a job you hate for your entire life. But I digress.

When you take all of this into account, it is easy to understand Seneca's argument that if we focused onthe most important things, life would be more than long enough.

For example, Abraham Lincoln was assassinated at age 56. Julius Caesar was assassinated as age 55. Napoleon died of stomach cancer at age 51. John F. Kennedy was assassinated at age 46. Alexander the Great died of poisoning at age 32.

Despite their premature deaths, nobody would dare argue that they didn't have enough time — that their lives were too short. Far from it.

The reason these men got so much done in so little time is that they focused on only the most important things. No Facebook. No television. No working to build someone else's dreams their entire life. No excessive time spent on email. No chasing shiny objects or wasting their life on distractions.

As Stephen Covey would say, these men "put first things first" and kept "the main thing the main thing." And it is for this reason that they achieved all that they did.

When it comes to striving to better manage our time and be more productive, there is a lot we can learn from these men.

### Concentrate Your Forces

*"Conserve your forces and energies by keeping them concentrated at their strongest point. You gain more by finding a rich mine and mining it deeper, than by flitting from one shallow mine to another—intensity defeats extensity every time. When looking for sources of power to elevate you, find the one key patron, the fat cow who will give you milk for a long time to come."*
*— Robert Greene, Law #23 from "The 48 Laws of Power"*

Napoleon Bonaparte was one of history's greatest generals. He conquered much of continental Europe and built an empire. Despite the immensity of his achievements, all of his success can be traced back to one simple principle: Concentrate one's forces.

As Napoleon said in his own words:

*"There are in Europe many good generals, but they see too many things at once. I see only **one thing**, namely the enemy's main body. I try to crush it, confident that secondary matters will then settle themselves."*

Rather than spread his army out and attacking the enemy evenly, he would throw the mass of his army against the decisive point. One notable way in which he did this was by having a small force hold off the flank. The small size of this force meant they couldn't overwhelmed the much larger enemy flank, but just hold them at bay. Meanwhile, the rest—the bulk—of Napoleon's army would attack the enemy's main force, and thus outnumber them at the battle's decisive point.

Demonstrating this once again in his own words, Napoleon said:

*"Fire must be concentrated on **one point**, and as soon as the breach is made, the equilibrium is broken and the rest is nothing."*

Blitzkrieg

*"The battlefront disappeared, and with it the illusion that there had ever been a battlefront. For this was no war of occupation, but a war of quick penetration and obliteration — Blitzkrieg, Lightning War."*
*— Unknown "TIME" Magazine Writer, September 25th, 1939*

Nazi Germany's most successful military strategy — blitzkrieg — took this same approach of concentrating one's forces. The blitzkrieg method of warfare has the "attacking force spearheaded by a **dense concentration** of armoured and motorised or mechanised infantry formations with close air support, break through the opponent's line of defence by short, fast, powerful attacks." (Thanks Wikipedia!)

Once again, the blitzkrieg strategy is based on the fact that, as Robert Greene wrote in *The 48 Laws of Power*, "intensity defeats extensity every time."

When it comes to time management, this strategy is essential. Applying the blitzkrieg strategy to time management literally enables you to get more done in less time.

Imagine how much longer it would have taken Nazi Germany and Napoleon to conquer continental Europe (if they succeeded at all) had they used the typical spread out, unfocused approach to battle.

Focusing, concentrating your forces, and prioritizing. These are essential to effective time management.

<u>Say No</u>

*"You have to decide what your highest priorities are and have the courage — pleasantly, smilingly, nonapologetically — to say 'no' to other things. And the way to do that is by having a bigger 'yes' burning inside."*
*— Stephen Covey*

Imagine a general and his army are advancing on the capital city of a country they are conquering. This capital city also serves as the enemy's main base, and so capturing this city will lead to certain victory. As such, this is the single most important thing. This is their main objective. Their ultimate goal.

As the army is advancing on the city, a small group of villagers from a little town a while away beg the general leading the army to help restore order in their village. According to the villagers, the outbreak of war has led to overwhelming looting and chaos in their town.

Confronted with the villagers pleading for help, the general has two choices: Go help restore order for the villagers and possibly delay his advance, or leave the villagers to fend for themselves and instead choose to focus exclusively on his main objective.

Ask yourself, if you were this general, what would your decision be?

It's pretty clear, isn't it? Of course you would choose to focus on the most important thing. Furthermore, if you were to evaluate this situation using the Eisenhower Matrix (incidentally, Eisenhower was also a general, ending up as Supreme Commander of the Allied Forces during World War II), the decision becomes even more clear.

Capturing the country's capital city is the Princess Luna of the situation, while the request of the villagers if the stormtrooper of the situation.

As Paulo Coelho advices, "When you say 'yes' to others, make sure you are not saying 'no' to yourself."

Apparently agreeing with this sentiment, Steve Jobs once said, "It's only by saying 'no' that you can concentrate on the things that are really important."

Unfortunately, most people far too often say "yes" to time consuming requests that really aren't that important. Even worse, you end up wasting time that could have been spent progressing toward the achievement of your most important goals. Clearly, this is terrible time management that will decrease your productivity, prevent you from doing the most important things, and impede your success.

## Time Blocks

Studies have found that 41 percent of tasks put on to-do lists never get completed. Put simply, you might as well toss a coin and that would pretty much determine whether a certain task on your to-do list gets done. Obviously, this is by no means an effective way to work.

The main problem with to-do lists is that they are ridiculously long (remember, intensity defeats extensity, not the other way around). Moreover, most of these tasks are not actually all that important.

Although it may seem deeply counterintuitive, doing less is actually far more efficient. Simply bouncing from one minor, unimportant task to another — just skimming across the top, doing very shallow work — is incredibly inefficient. Focusing intensely on no more than one to three highly important tasks, diving deep and doing high quality work as a result, is actually the best way to work smart. Not only will you complete all your important tasks, but they will be done in less time and at a higher quality.

The key to it all is this: Less volume, more time. Eliminate the nonessential and unimportant, and spend more time on the things that actually matter — that move you toward your biggest goals.

Most people spend — no, *waste* — so much time on unimportant miscellaneous activities that simply buckling down on only a few very important tasks sees their productivity go through the roof. It is honestly one of the best time management strategies there is.

<u>Airplane Days</u>

A wide variety of people, from CEOs to novelists, have reported being ultra-productive on airplane flights. Is it because airplanes have some special scent or produce a certain noise that puts our brains into a highly productive state?

Of course not!

The reason people get so much done is because they have a set block of time during which they can't do anything else. It's time management on steroids.

They can't go anywhere. There's nobody dropping in to bother you. There's no phone calls or text messages. No cat videos. No Facebook or Twitter notifications.

It's just you and your work.

Fortunately, you don't need to drop several thousands bucks to go on an international flight in order to experience this. All you need to do is block out a day (or half-day) on your calendar, get out of the office, and put (and keep!) all your devices on airplane mode.1

Furthermore, if you combine the "airplane days" method with another time management strategy, such as the Ivy Lee Method, you'll be getting so much done that you won't believe it.

So block out some time and work smart!

<u>The Calendar vs. the To-Do List</u>

Earlier, it was mentioned that studies show that 41 percent of tasks put on to-do lists never get done. Not only does this demonstrate how ineffective to-do lists are, but it is indicative of a more serious symptom: Most people don't prioritize.

One of the major pitfalls of the typical to-do list is that it shows neither the importance nor the urgency of tasks.

But what is the alternative?

Well, there's another way, and it is far more effective at managing your time (in no small part due to the fact it literally measures time). Meet *the calendar.*

Do you think presidents of the United States, Steve Jobs, or Elon Musk use to-do list? Of course they don't! What they do instead is keep a schedule. If they realize they need to do something, they schedule it.

Keeping a schedule not only ensures that you get whatever it is you schedule done (you've set time aside to do it, after all), but it forces you to prioritize. It confronts you with the fact that you only have so many hours in a day.

If you want to turbocharge your schedule, combine it with the "McDonald's system" method discussed earlier.

All that being said, though, calendars do have one negative — they're not as flexible as a to-do list. However, this can also be an advantage for, as you procrastinators out there will know, too much flexibility can lead to getting nothing done.

Nonetheless, it is best to keep a certain degree of flexibility. Be a little on the conservative side when estimating how long it will take to get things done, and don't organize your schedule in five minute intervals or you'll regularly end up being forced to abandon it.

# Chapter 5: Engineer Your Day

So far, we've discussed many time management techniques. Two of these included how to take a "divide and conquer" approach to your work and why you should determine what you need to do each evening (or morning).

Now we'll discuss specific ways to structure your time for maximum effectiveness, as well as how you can utilize these time management strategies to guarantee you get things done.

Let's get started with some ways to approach each day.

## The Pomodoro Technique

The pomodoro technique — a time management hack popular amongst productivity gurus — was devised by an Italian named Francesco Cirillo in the late 1980s. Cirillo would divide his work up into short sprints of intense productivity followed by brief breaks. Each one of these short work sessions became known as a "pomodoro"—

named after the tomato-shaped kitchen timer he used to time these work sessions. (In Italian, the work "pomodoro" means tomato).

Here's a quick run-down on how the pomodoro technique works:

1. Set a timer for 25 minutes and do 100 percent focused, uninterrupted work until the timer rings. If you get distracted, you must start the entire pomodoro again. The best way to avoid the temptation of distraction is to make a "distraction to-do list" on which you write down whatever you felt the urge to do—whether it be read the news, check Facebook, or browse Reddit. You can do these later.

2. After your 25-minute pomodoro, take a 3–5 minute break.

3. After a brief break lasting no more than five minutes, do another pomodoro.

4. After completing four pomodoros (i.e. four 25-minute intensely focused work sessions divided by five-minute breaks), take a longer break of 15–30 minutes.

5. Repeat this process as many times as needed.

The pomodoro technique has many benefits. First up, it keeps you focused and refreshed. But it also—and perhaps more importantly in the context of time management—can be a highly effective system to break down your day. Using the pomodoro technique, you can reverse engineer tasks and projects to ensure that they get done.

Here's how.

Start off by determining what needs to be done. You could use the Ivy Lee method, the Eisenhower Matrix, or any other approach that ensures the tasks you complete yield the plentiful results you're after.

After having determined the most important things you could be doing, break them down into little steps. Divide and conquer.

Finally, plan your pomodoros (write out a basic schedule) and dedicate each pomodoro to a specific tasks—a "little step." What you are doing is utilizing the pomodoro technique to set yourself productivity targets and deadlines, the doing of which will inevitably boost productivity.

Let's explore yet another great—and perhaps more exciting—way to break down your day and get your most important tasks and projects done.

## Workstation Popcorn

Workstation popcorn, as a time management method, is highly effective as it puts not only the pressure of time and deadlines on you, but also of location.

Confused? Let's take a look at how it works.

The brainchild of Joel Runyon at ImpossibleHQ (http://impossiblehq.com/), workstation popcorn requires you to complete three tasks at three different locations.

Not only does that force you to prioritize, but the fact you need to move to a new location forces you to buckle down and get your work done. All of a sudden, your juicy Facebook notifications seem less appetizing.

For best results, assign one important tasks to each location and make sure the locations are around 30 minutes walk from each other. This will help refresh your mind and get the blood flowing. Furthermore, you can break down your different tasks for each of the locations into three sub-projects. Otherwise you could also just allocate three individual tasks (but no more than three) to each location to evenly spread out your workload. That being said, it is still a good idea to keep it as simple and focused as possible. You don't have time to do everything, but you do have time to do the most important things.

## Journaling

*"A life worth living is a life worth recording."*
*— Jim Rohn*

World-class athletes and bodybuilders almost universally keep a journal. And no, not a "Dear Diary" kind of journal.

They use their journals to set goals, record results, reflect, keep track of diet, adjust workouts and training sessions, and plan.

While you won't be journaling with the goal of running faster or lifting heavier weights, journaling can nonetheless prove to be invaluable. After all, your goals aren't actually all that different. You seek to work faster and lift heavier workloads. Not all that dissimilar, right?

You can use journaling to set long-term goals, short-term goals, and daily goals. In fact, in his book *The ONE Thing*, Gary Keller advises people to break down their goals as follows:

**LIFE GOAL:** Define your mission in life. The ONE Thing you wish to accomplish.

**FIVE-YEAR GOAL:** What is the ONE Thing that you can do in the next five years to help achieve your life goal?

**ONE-YEAR GOAL:** What is the ONE Thing that you can do this year to help achieve your five-year goal?

And then you do the same and create a monthly goal, weekly goal, daily goal, and finally, you can ask yourself, "What is the ONE Thing I can do right now to help achieve today's goal?"

This method of goal setting—of breaking down and reverse engineering your biggest and most ambitious goal(s)—is an excellent way to measure progress in your journal. A journal is also an excellent place to store ideas and quotes that motivate you. You can keep track of how you feel and reflect on what specific habits, settings, or actions make you more productive.

Take Ernest Hemingway for example—a man who was awarded the Nobel Prize (and the Pulitzer Prize) for his immense impact on 20th century literature. Hemingway kept journals for jotting down ideas, capturing the richness and texture of experiences, and even keeping track of the menstrual cycles of his first wife.

Most importantly, Hemingway would keep track of his productivity by counting and recording the number of words he wrote each day.

Many other famous men have kept journals for similar purposes, too—sans the menstrual cycles. Thomas Edison and Leonardo da Vinci used journals to keep track of ideas for inventions, and Beethoven for symphonies.

George C. Marshall, US Army Chief of Staff during World War II, famously used his journal to take note of promising candidates for future leadership positions—with such men as Eisenhower and Patton found mentioned in his notebook.

Similarly, George S. Patton used his journal to jot down affirmations and write down principles that would help him to achieve his ultimate goal of becoming a great general.

Here are some of them:

*"Do your damdest always."*

*"Always do more than is required of you."*

*"You can be what you* will *to be."*

He also wrote on the cover page of one of his notebooks, "SUCCESS IN WAR DEPENDS UPON THE GOLDEN RULE OF WAR: SPEED — SIMPLICITY — BOLDNESS."

Benjamin Franklin used a journal to keep track of his progress toward his ambitious goal of moral perfection. Using his journal, he developed a program to develop 13 virtues. Franklin would use his journal to evaluate his progress and record slip-ups, placing a dot next to the virtues he had violated. In later years, Franklin wrote, "I am indebted to my notebook for the happiness of my whole life."

Although your goal may not be one of achieving moral perfections, as Franklin's was, it is easy to see how you use much the same journaling technique to keep track of and work toward your own goals. In fact, one man did just that—and, to put it mildly, it worked out extremely well. He became one of the richest men to have ever walked the face of the earth.

John D. Rockefeller used a journal to jot down notes to himself, record ideas for making his business more efficient, write down facts and figures, and do calculations—all in his crusade to maximize efficiency.

All in all, there is a lot we can learn from the journaling habit of these great men. Journaling, even if utilized in only its most basic form, can prove invaluable. You can use journaling as a way of breaking down your goals, prioritizing, scheduling, keeping track of productivity, and recording results.

I discovered one particularly great—and yet simple—template for doing this at an old sales job I had. At the end of each day, everybody would open up their notebooks and draw up a two-by-two table—leaving four boxes in total. We would label one of the four boxes "Pitch," the next one "Pace," then "Attitude," and title the final box "Goals."

Under the first three headings—"Pitch", "Pace", "Attitude"—we would write three positives. Things we had done well that day. We would write it as a bullet point, but with a "+" rather than a dot point.

So for "Pitch" (as in sales pitch), one positive might have written, "Today I used funny icebreakers that put potential customers at ease." Or, "I am getting better at doing hard closes by assuming the sale."

We would then do the same in the "Pace" box (as in speed—did we go fast and pitch lots of potential customers or did we go at a slow, leisurely pace and not talk to many people?) and the "Attitude" box (attitude as in where we grumpy and bored or excited and enthusiastic when dealing with potential customers?).

We would then write in our notebooks three negatives for each of the first three headings (Pitch, Pace, and Attitude). Things we didn't do so well that day. Things we could improve on. We would write these as bullet points, but with a "-" rather than a dot point.

Once we had written down three positives and negatives for each of these sections, we would then turn our attention to the one remaining empty box in our two-by-two tables: "Goals."

In this section, we would write out three goals for tomorrow. Things we could improve on. We would then focus on these goals the next day—one goal in the morning, the next during the middle of the day, and the final goal in the afternoon. This would ensure that we were always improving and getting better.

Although you probably won't use this exact template (unless you're a salesperson, that is!), hopefully this has given you insight into just one example of an effective way to go about journaling.

You can also alter this template to fit your goal needs. For example, a journalist or writer might replace "Pitch" with "Quality" and write three positives and negatives about the quality, style, and readability of their writing that day, and whether or not their writing is information and engaging.

They could do the same for "Pace" (e.g. did the words flow or were they stuck?), and "Attitude" (you'd be surprised at how much you attitude impacts your work, no matter what industry you're in).

Based on this brief yet comprehensive analysis of their day's work, they could then write three goals—things on which to improve—for the next day. For example, writing seven percent more words and beginning articles with a captivating first sentence.

No matter your type of work, journaling is a highly effective way of continuously improving the quality and quantity of your output. Moreover, you can use journaling as the glue that connects all these time management strategies together—from daily goal setting and the Ivy Lee Method to the Eisenhower Matrix, from the "McDonald's system" to reverse engineering your day using the pomodoro technique or workstation popcorn, to even writing down your schedule and scheduling some ultra-productive "airplane days."

# Chapter 6: Daily Routines

*"Be regular and orderly in your life, so that you may be violent and original in your work."*
*— Gustave Flaubert*

Woody Allen once famously said that "80 percent of success is showing up."

This is one of the truest statements you'll ever encounter.

A bodybuilder who works out for 30 minutes every single day without fail will build far more muscle than a bodybuilder who sporadically goes to the gym, if he feels motivated, and does a five-hour workout on these rare occasions.

A write who consistently rises early and produces 1,000 words every single morning without fail will be far more successful than a writer who, every now and then, writes ten thousand words in a sudden burst of motivation.

A person seeking to lose weight who consistently chooses water over soda and vegetables over chips and donuts will lose far more weight than someone who occasionally attempts an extreme diet before promptly quitting when the desired results don't instantly materialize.

An entrepreneur who, without fail, spends 60 minutes each day reading books and listening to audio programs to learn as much as he possibly can about dominating his industry and amplifying the success of his business will end up far more successful than a fellow entrepreneur who only occasionally reads a book or learns about their industry and business when feeling "inspired."

An employed professional who religiously adheres to the same practice of 60 minutes of learning about his industry will similarly end up a leading industry expert and find themselves highly valued and, as a result, highly paid.

As Bruce lee once said, "Long-term consistently beats short-term intensity."

And when it come to developing a habit of long-lasting consistently, there is no better route to take than that of developing an efficient daily routine.

There are many things we do every day that are essential to our success. Whether that be working out, writing a thousand words, or becoming an expert in your field, a well-developed daily routine can prove to be the greatest time management strategy at your disposal.

Demonstrating this point is the morning ritual of the prolific writer Anthony Trollope. Trollope is perhaps the greatest example of the effectiveness of a well-developed daily routine.

In his fantastic book, *Daily Rituals: How Artists Work*, Mason Currey writes, "A solid routine fosters a well-worn groove for one's mental energies and helps stave off the tyranny of moods."

So let's take a look at just one example, that of Anthony Trollope.

Each morning, Trollope rose at 5am, writing from 5:30am to 8:30am. Trollope describes his morning ritual in *Autobiography*:

*"It had at this time become my custom--and it still is my custom, though of late I have become a little lenient to myself--to write with my watch before me, and to require from myself 250 words every quarter of an hour. I have found that the 250 words have been forthcoming as regularly as my watch went."*

These timed writing sessions were undoubtedly the key to Trollope's prolific output.

Writing about this ridiculously efficient approach to time management, Trollope wrote the following:

*"This division of time allowed me to produce over ten pages of an ordinary novel volume a day, and if kept up through ten months, would have given as its results three novels of three volumes each in the year."*

After completing his three hours of writing at a pace of 250 words every 15 minutes, Trollope would head off to his day job with the postal service.

To give you an idea of how strict his routine was, consider the fact that if Trollope finished a novel before his session finished at 8:30am, he would simply take out a fresh sheet of paper and start his next book immediately.

And Trollope isn't the only person to find great success with such a method of time management.

Nobel Prize winning writer Ernest Hemingway, as mentioned earlier, would record his daily word count on a chart "so as not to kid myself." Also a fan of accountability metrics was B. F. Skinner—the famed psychologist, behaviorist, inventor, and social philosopher—who would start and stop his work sessions with the setting of a timer, "and carefully plotted the number of hours" he worked and the output he produced.

Another key reason—in addition to having accountability metrics—that Trollope's time management strategy is just so damn effective is that he had a clear dividing line that separated his work from other activities.

Without a clear starting and—more importantly—stopping point, we end up wasting time and not working as efficiently as we could be. When we know exactly when we finish, close our laptop, and get up, we work much more efficiently and productively during that work session.

Consistency is the key. Developing a highly precise and unfailingly consistent daily routine is perhaps the single most effective time management "hack" their is.

As Gustave Flaubert said, "Be regular and orderly in life, so that you may be violent and original in your work."

Or, as Anthony Trollope, the role model for this time management technique, wrote, "A small daily task, if it be really daily, will beat the labours of a spasmodic Hercules."

# Conclusion

Time management is to productivity what strategy is to warfare. Continuing this analogy, I hope this book has equipped you with an arsenal of battle plans and tactics that will ensure great victories and enable you to conquer your most ambitious goals.

Made in the USA
Las Vegas, NV
13 December 2020

12810634R00035